NEXT-LEVEL INCLUSIONIST

Transform Your Work and Yourself for
Diversity, Equity, and Inclusion Success

DR. NIKA WHITE

Next-Level Inclusionist

Transform Your Work and Yourself for Diversity, Equity, and Inclusion Success

Dr. Nika White

This book is dedicated to all diversity and inclusion practitioners, inequity disruptors, and leaders who commit every day to stay on course to create more equitable and inclusive societies. Although our experience can feel lonely at times, let us celebrate small wins, support each other, and remain encouraged. Sometimes we are planting seeds, and other times we are directly changing minds and behaviors. Whatever the individual journey calls for, it is our collective will, passion, and effort that moves us toward a world in which everyone can do their best work and live their best lives. Day in and day out, we are walking this road together.

Contents

Introduction

It's time to move to the next level.

Some of you holding this book in your hands are at the beginning of your journey toward creating a more diverse and inclusive organization. Even if diversity and inclusion (D&I) is not in your job title, you're looking for the next step to increase your knowledge and build skills that will help you create a more inclusive environment wherever you wield your influence.

Others of you have been doing this noble and challenging work for some time. You've faced and overcome obstacles to your efforts to create a more inclusive organization. You've also found yourself at times stalled, uninspired, or simply out of new ideas.

To leaders at both stages – and everywhere in between – I'm excited you are answering the call to become an Intentional Inclusionist®. It's the term I have coined for those of us who see being inclusion-minded as an integral part of leadership and who work with passion, purpose, and intentionality. It means we are proactive in creating an atmosphere where people can reach their full potential. It means we're grossly unsatisfied with the status quo and willing to push ourselves, our practice, and our organizations to make D&I a reality in our sphere of influence.

Consider this book a toolkit that will help you change your perspective, your work, your results, and yourself. With a deeper understanding of emerging principles such as equity and intersectionality and mastery of tactical methods to increase impact, generate buy-in, and recondition your own thinking, practitioners at any level can maximize their results.

THE CHANGING LANDSCAPE

Taking a broader view for just a moment, let's look at the "why" of an intentional approach to D&I. The truth is, we are in the midst of a critical era for D&I.

Across sectors, organizations are being swept up by the rising tide of interest in having some level of D&I activity. Social and political issues are causing leaders to step up by either introducing or improving D&I initiatives. Even so, research and anecdotal evidence reveal a number of challenges to D&I work today that an intentional approach can help address.

Too many existing diversity programs are failing to produce diverse, inclusive, and equitable environments. The *Harvard Business Review* reported recently that while "U.S. companies spend millions annually on diversity programs and policies . . . [from] ensuring equal employment opportunity compliance, to instituting cultural sensitivity training programs, to focusing on the recruitment and retention of minorities and women . . . they are not increasing demographic diversity, and may even be decreasing it."[1]

At the same time, the landscape in which this work is being done is changing rapidly. Among the most pressing concerns are:

- **Changing demographics** in the United States and around the world are causing the makeup of our workplaces to shift incredibly quickly, challenging longstanding cultures and power structures within organizations.

- An **increased generational mix**, fueled by a rising retirement age and exploding youth population, means an unprecedented range of age groups are negotiating the workplace together.

- The **ongoing war for top talent** is forcing organizations to consider new pools for recruiting and retaining employees.

- **Client and customer expectations** have spread beyond service and product delivery to a concern about company culture and social responsibility.

- **Growing multiracial** and other identity categories are exposing difference in new ways and forcing new thinking about D&I.

- **Complex social issues** can directly impact whether employees can show up as their best at work.

Those of us who are up for meeting these challenges through D&I practice must embrace the truth that doing the work the same way it's been done for decades won't suffice. It's time for us to redefine success, both for ourselves and for our organizations.

Next-Level Leadership

I remember when I first started working in this space and assumed the role of Vice President of Diversity. Sitting in a room with about eight of the organization's leaders — chief diversity officers, board members, the president, and others — I put my stake in the ground. I told the group, "If you're looking to hire a diversity and inclusion cop, I'm not your person. But if you're looking for strategic thought leadership that can bring value from a business perspective to help the organization reach its mission, then I am your person for this job."

I'd hoped to set a high bar for myself and for the organization because I believe that's what is needed in our work. Now, as head of my own consulting firm, my aim is to empower other leaders with a vision of the deep and lasting change D&I can make in any organization and the powerful shifts we can experience with new tools and perspectives to do our work.

At this important time in history, leaders of all stripes should be setting a higher bar for enabling diverse, equitable, and inclusive workplaces. D&I cannot be only the responsibility of human resources professionals or individuals with D&I in their titles. The true leaders are emerging from the ranks of those who see beyond their titles, taking an inclusion-minded view of leadership at every stage of their careers.

Wherever you are today, I encourage you to push your work to the next level. The tools included in this book will be a practical resource to revisit often and a source of strength as you do this important work.

Chapter 1
Supercharge Your Mind

In industries across the country, diversity and inclusion (D&I) efforts are missing their mark. One of the key challenges goes much deeper than the programs, resources, or structures that D&I practitioners face. However, even those most dedicated to D&I can be hampered by habitual ways of thinking that limit the maximum effectiveness of their D&I efforts.

The stark reality: The problem with your D&I efforts might be you.

Practitioners at all levels often ask themselves, *Why won't people engage? Why don't our programs work? Why isn't this work more effective?*

A powerful tool can address this problem: mindfulness.

Being inclusion-minded is a leadership function. It should directly impact our attitudes, the ways in which we lead, the ways in which we interact with others. Assuming a true leadership role in D&I requires going beyond the basics to become an Intentional Inclusionist®. It requires a deep understanding of the personal and workplace impacts of exclusion – and that requires mindfulness.

So, how can mindfulness supercharge our D&I work? Mastering the skill of focusing our minds unlocks numerous capabilities:

- We can cultivate an ability to reflect on the experiences of others at critical times.

- We can train our minds to be more aware of potential conflicts and the hidden impacts of our work where they relate to D&I.

- We can get better at managing (up or down) to attain needed levels of support for D&I efforts.

- We can learn to unpack myths about D&I and better evaluate incoming information.

- We can help manage expectations and repress our own urge to "fix it and move on" when D&I work reveals a complex problem without a quick or easy solution.

- We can become better and more compassionate change managers due to heightened awareness.

In short, a mindful approach adds a great deal of value to people working as allies and advocates for D&I. If you don't intentionally include, you will unintentionally exclude. As we work every day, we face conscious and subconscious obstacles from ourselves and others; adopting a mindful approach is key to meeting those challenges. More importantly, it offers you the opportunity to develop a new way of thinking about the work of inclusion that can energize your work and maximize your results.

CHANGING YOUR MIND

In doing D&I work, we're bringing our own mental conditioning to the table. For most of us, that includes some habits and attitudes we need to mindfully correct before we can do our most impactful work. Consider the following common obstacles and whether you've noticed any of them appear in your thinking as you examine or perform your work.

1. The Fix-It-and-Move-On Mentality
D&I practitioners and the people they answer to often want a checklist of problems and solutions to work through. Yet, this work often requires deep changes and long-term work, making it hard to stay enthusiastic and sustain the momentum needed to achieve successive goals. The result can be initiatives that don't hit the mark or efforts that remain permanently stalled by the desire for a one-size-fits-all solution.

2. Masking Problems
Diversity initiatives can fail for a number of reasons. One study found that while diversity initiatives aim to improve outcomes for low-status groups in organizations, they might actually make it

harder to detect discrimination.[2] Essentially, people tend to believe that once an organization introduces diversity initiatives, the problems disappear. Or, as the case tends to be, people become less vigilant and less likely to detect discrimination.[3]

3. Failing to Consider All Groups

D&I practitioners can be blind to the impacts that activities and messaging have on all groups – both advantaged and disadvantaged. For example, pro-diversity messages have been found to signal to white men that they might be undervalued and discriminated against. This response showed itself as physical stress symptoms and reduced performance scores on job interviews irrespective of the men's political ideologies, attitudes toward minorities, beliefs about fairness, or even avowed support for diversity.

4. Outdated Thinking

Authors Frank Dobbin and Alexandra Kalev noted in 2017 that many diversity programs are failing to adapt to the changing social and professional landscape. They wrote, "Despite a few new bells and whistles, courtesy of big data, companies are basically doubling down on the same approaches they've used since the 1960s – which often make things worse, not better."[4] With renewed minds, we can thoughtfully question whether an initiative or activity truly solves today's problems in the way our organization needs.

GETTING INTENTIONAL, MINDFULLY

An intentional approach, beginning with mindfulness, can help D&I practitioners avoid the kinds of costly pitfalls described in the previous section. But, what is mindfulness? The most widely used definition is "intentional, non-judgmental awareness of moment-to-moment experience."[5] In recent decades, mindfulness practices, which have been based in stress reduction and improving well-being, have penetrated the business world for tackling a number of issues.

Managing yourself means being mindful and self-aware. These are the attributes of leaders who have the propensity to practice intentional inclusion consistently. When we are not mindful, we compromise our ability to be intentional. It's easy to approach a situation with an unconscious bias when we are simply unaware. Lack of awareness creates blind spots that can lead to exclusion.

On the other hand, beginning with mindfulness enables practitioners to:

- approach diversity work with new perspectives,
- determine and perform the personal work needed to strengthen diversity practices,
- better understand diversity challenges on multiple levels,
- become change agents who recognize the difference between equality and equity,
- engage in respectful questioning and become a student of human difference,
- be proactive in finding ways to create space for all to contribute and feel valued,

- become comfortable respectfully challenging existing practices,

- recognize the need to minimize both people bias and process bias,

- understand the difference between activity versus impact,

- unpack myths about D&I, and

- better evaluate information as it comes rather than accepting or rejecting it wholesale.

CRACKING TOUGH TOPICS

There are some topics the people we work with feel they simply cannot wrap their minds around. Often, the real issue is a mental block that won't allow them to accept new information.

For example, the concept of privilege is something a lot of people have a hard time accepting, especially groups such as white men, who tend to have greater advantages in our society. With mindfulness, this group can better see their place as part of a whole and how that relationship impacts others.

On the other hand, there's an automatic negative reaction to the idea that white men also can experience disadvantages despite their often-privileged status. In this case, members of commonly disadvantaged groups can lack empathy or even refuse to acknowledge the disadvantages of those they perceive to be privileged.

I have had a white male raise his hand in one of my consulting sessions and say, "I know that there are a lot of things that I don't have to necessarily think about, that maybe other marginalized groups have to think about, and so in that regard I am privileged, but I also grew up with humble beginnings. I was not even aware on certain days if I would be able to eat a certain meal."

At the same time, members of marginalized groups can fail to recognize the privilege they do enjoy in some contexts. Even as an African-American woman, I have to be mindful of being well and able-bodied, not to mention having grown up with more than enough materially and having continual access to higher education. It can be a great mental leap for some people to broaden their thinking about privilege, but I truly believe that all of us have a certain level of privilege if we were to honestly take inventory of our lives.

In all cases, mindfulness is key to having more than just a superficial understanding of others, breaking down mental barriers that keep stereotypes alive.

How Mindfulness Works

Mindfulness helps directly address unconscious bias, the automatic or "knee-jerk" reactions we have without thinking.

Oppression occurs when one acts on misinformation about an individual or a particular group with the intent to limit their opportunities. We all record misinformation about people who are different than we are. No one is born with bias or bigotry; rather, certain thoughts and behaviors are learned or transferred based upon experience of another group – whether heard in a casual conversation, read in the newspaper, seen in the media, or gleaned from everyday life – and stored within as a record.

These records stay with us even when the information contradicts what we come to believe. Even as truths are revealed, earlier misinformation is not easily erased. Instead, it continues to exert a powerful, often unrecognized influence on our thoughts and actions. Our brains unconsciously make decisions based on what feels safe, likeable, valuable, and competent. Unconscious beliefs impact the way we perceive others and ultimately impact our actions at work.

Thankfully, there are several ways mindfulness helps counteract these innate tendencies and behaviors:

- Research has shown that mindfulness reduces implicit age and race bias. This worked even when people were taught mindfulness techniques just a few minutes before being assessed.[6]

- In some instances, not only are people able to reduce their implicit bias, but they can even become more aware when they've already made the mistake.[7]

- Meditation, one of several mindfulness practices, can increase compassionate responses to others' suffering and decrease implicit bias against stigmatized groups.[8] This helps D&I practitioners as social and workplace landscapes change and new categories of underserved populations emerge.

- One study suggests that "even a brief mindfulness-related instruction can implicitly reduce the propensity to perpetuate stereotypical thinking through language."[9]

When you are mindful, you are more self-aware of your actions, your thoughts, and how you may be presenting yourself to others. This leads to a greater capacity to identify those times when our actions impede inclusion. Mindfulness also causes us to take inventory of the actions, behaviors, and attitudes of those around us, which leads to an opportunity to influence those behaviors in such a way that inclusion can be fostered. This requires situational awareness and intentionality.

When you can better manage yourself,
then you can better manage and lead others.

GETTING STARTED WITH MINDFULNESS PRACTICES

Mindfulness takes practice, just as D&I work does. Below are two activities for getting started.[10]

#1 BECOMING AWARE (5-10 MINUTES EACH)

1. Pay attention.

The next time you meet someone new or encounter somebody you know, listen closely to his or her words. Think about their meaning and uniqueness. Aim to develop a habit of understanding others and delaying your own judgments and criticisms.

2. Make the familiar new again.

Find a few small, familiar objects — such as a toothbrush, an apple, or a cellphone — in your home or office. Look at the objects with fresh eyes. Identify one new detail about each object that you didn't see before. As you become more aware of your world, you may become fonder of the things around you.

3. Focus on your breathing.

Sit in a quiet place with your back straight but relaxed. Feel your breath move in and out of your body. Let your awareness of everything else fall away. Pay attention to your nostrils as air passes in and out and how your abdomen expands and collapses with each breath. When your mind wanders, gently redirect your attention to the act of breathing. Don't judge yourself. Remember that you're not trying to become anything, such as a good meditator. You're simply becoming aware of what's happening around you, breath by breath.

> *Awareness leads to mindfulness, mindfulness to intentionality,*
> *and intentionality to lasting success.*

#2 TAMING THE CRITIC (30 MINUTES)

1. Examine criticisms.

If you allow critical judgments to remain unexamined, they can come to occupy your thoughts, emotions, and even your dreams. But if you examine them, you'll find patterns that are connected to life events and discover that even your judgments regarding others are often rooted in self-judgment or events that happened earlier in your life – sometimes when you were very young. It's a good practice to investigate all of your judgments, and this practice will help you do exactly that. Give yourself about 30 minutes for this inquiry.

2. Recall a judgment.

Next, see if you can remember a strong judgment you've had about yourself or someone else in the last few days.

3. Take note of the sensations in the body.

As you feel into the judgment, notice whether there's a physical component – something you feel in your body. Spend a few minutes investigating the way your body feels as you reflect on this judgment.

4. Explore the thoughts that accompany the judgment.

Was there anything automatic in the way this judgment came up? For example, was the judgment a reaction to something or someone? Spend at least five minutes investigating the thoughts that arise in relation to this judgment.

5. Explore the emotions that accompany the judgment.

For example, some judgments may call forth anger, whereas others evoke shame and yet others evoke compassion. Spend some time investigating the emotions that arise in relation to this judgment.

6. Notice your observing mind.

Notice that the part of you that is investigating this judgment is not itself judging anything; it's simply observing bodily sensations, thoughts, and emotions with balance and curiosity.

7. Recall whether this kind of judgment has come up before.

Does it come up often? If so, do you have any sense of why you have this strong and automatic reaction? Does it isolate you from others or make you feel more connected? Can you sense where it comes from? Spend a few minutes reflecting on the historical associations related to this judgment.

8. Write about some of the ideas that surfaced.

Take a little time to write about what came up for you as you investigated your judgments. What sorts of physical sensations and emotions were associated with different judgments? Did you discover any associations between judgments and earlier life events?

Moving Forward Mindfully

Although habitual thinking can get in the way of maximum effectiveness for our D&I work, a mindful approach can break through those habits. By training the mind with simple mindfulness practices, you are able to sharpen your awareness and work with intentionality.

A mindful approach adds a great deal of value to people working as allies and advocates for D&I. It improves your ability to manage yourself and short-circuit automatic reactions that might be impacting the way you work. What's more, it increases your receptivity and understanding of others and recognition of what is happening in the moment.

Mindfulness also causes us to take inventory of the actions, behaviors, and attitudes of those around us, which leads to an opportunity to influence those behaviors in such a way that inclusion can be fostered. That makes D&I work become more impactful, and therefore more enjoyable.

You must have the right mindset for inclusion and belonging, for if you don't intentionally include, you will unintentionally exclude.

Chapter 2
Secrets to Winning Buy-In

Sometimes D&I practitioners forget how much we need others to get our work done. Even after mastering important concepts and adopting game-changing tools, we must still create strategic partnerships across different stakeholder groups if we're going to make any meaningful change. That's simply the reality of our situation.

Not only do we have to reach out, but we might also even have to lead from the sidelines. In the best-case scenario, you'll have a cadre of other people to be the voices and faces of the work. That means that they are being influenced by your work, owning the message for themselves, and becoming more likely to help execute the work. What's more, they'll help serve as the ambassadors who can bring others along as well.

While D&I has become at least part of normal business discussion in many organizations, practitioners still face significant challenges when it comes time to get the necessary people involved. It's one thing for people within an organization to tolerate D&I initiatives, but it's another when they become active supporters. Real change happens when stakeholders buy in.

Getting buy-in can be an enormous challenge for several reasons. As previously discussed, rapidly changing demographics in the United States and worldwide are increasingly reflected in our workplaces. Organizations are seeing more generations, ethnicities, and races working together than ever before. Additionally, multiracial and other identity categories are being recognized, sometimes revealing even more barriers to inclusion.

As a result of this complexity, the lone wolf D&I champion is rarely if ever successful. However, it is the responsibility of D&I leaders to help others in their organizations understand the importance of the work and the roles that everyone can play in moving it forward.

WHO NEEDS TO "BUY IN"?

Buy-in spans the spectrum of participation from engaged openness to advocacy. Various levels of buy-in are needed from one stakeholder group to another and from the ground level of the organization to the top. What's more, this includes both internal and external stakeholders.

In some cases, buy-in might require you to "manage up," or guide your superiors, or learn to be strategic. While much D&I program conversation revolves around the experiences of rank-and-file employees, other groups who might require special attention and strategies include organization leaders, managers, and constituent groups.

- **Leadership** – the top levels of an organization – are crucial for successful cultural shifts that address D&I problems within an organization. These include the C-suite, high-level managers, and organizational boards. Any directional change within an organization that has lasting, widespread impact comes from the top. As a D&I practitioner, these might not be the first people you engage in your work, but they are undoubtedly the most important to show that D&I are truly being embraced as a priority. As a result, leadership buy-in looks like enthusiastic official endorsement of all activities related to D&I and the designation of appropriate resources for accomplishing its stated goals.

- **Managers** are often at the front lines of D&I implementation. They are the ones who have to respond to staff who might be uncomfortable with changes, and they often are responsible for ensuring that change happens. Sometimes, it's the managers themselves who are being asked to make the most radical changes in mindset and behavior. They might be looking for validation that such demands are not personal. They also need clear justifications in order to motivate themselves and other employees to participate and, hopefully, embrace D&I initiatives.

- **Clients and customers** might also be a group whose support you will need. This may include other organizations, partners, donors, or individual consumers. The societal factors that drive D&I are operating everywhere. If customers become aware of an organization's D&I by being directly informed or by indirectly noticing, they might be inclined to respond. It is the D&I practitioner's responsibility to anticipate where resistance might crop up and head it off with appropriate information and opportunities for engagement.

Unfortunately, too many bad diversity programs have helped fortify negative perceptions of work that can be difficult even under the best circumstances. A survey by Novations/J. Howard & Associates, a Boston, Massachusetts, D&I consulting firm, illustrates this point well.[11]

Among the findings, attitudes feeding resistance to D&I initiatives included the following:

- Many employees, including women and other minority groups, think corporate diversity programs benefit only black employees.

- Of 1,134 employees surveyed, 47 percent of whites, 50 percent of Asians and Native Americans, and 53 percent of Hispanics believed "only some groups" have benefited from a focus on diversity.

- Blacks are much less likely than whites (37 percent versus 62 percent) to believe that their executive management's goals or actions reflect a real commitment to diversity.

Lack of clarity is another major challenge to buy-in. When people cannot clearly see the benefits to themselves or their organization, or when they're not sure exactly what is expected of them, they are reluctant to support or actively enable change. D&I leaders need to equip stakeholders to understand and communicate the drivers for D&I, within both their organization and the larger societal contexts.

The following are six secrets to countering the negative perceptions, misconceptions, and execution mistakes that keep people from getting on board with D&I initiatives.

#1 TALK BUSINESS

Whatever the "business" of your organization, a strong business case carries a lot of weight with stakeholders of all categories. It's crucial that everyone understands how D&I can help your organization do its work better. No matter the nature of the organization, be it corporate or nonprofit, all stakeholders need to understand how D&I will help better achieve its stated mission and goals.

Lisa Wilson, deputy director of human resources for the city of Columbus, Ohio, and past chair of the Workplace Diversity

Committee for the Society for Human Resource Management (SHRM), put the approach succinctly for that group: "We're now looking at a whole different picture. Diversity is no longer only a social mandate; it is also a competitive advantage."[12]

Thankfully, a solid body of supportive research spanning multiple years and multiple industries shows this to be the case. Everything from bottom-line growth to talent retention has been a direct result of D&I initiatives. We know this research demonstrates a correlation between workforce diversity and company profits, and that available data will be your friend in making this argument, especially to leadership.

Furthermore, customers, clients, and other constituent groups expect organizations to deal equitably with diverse groups. The younger generations that are growing up and making decisions about which organizations they want to support are increasingly prioritizing diversity. Generation Z, for instance, born after 1996, is not only the most diverse age group in America, but also the most inclusive. They are less likely to label others and are more accepting of fluid identities, and they expect the same from others.

#2 REDEFINE LEADERSHIP

Inclusiveness is more than a goal or an activity; in today's world, it's a leadership necessity. In fact, Deloitte, the international consulting firm known for forecasting business trends, delineates four global mega-trends — diversity of markets, customers, ideas, and talent — that are pushing organizations toward clarifying and prioritizing inclusive leadership.[13] As a D&I practitioner, you can make great strides by helping managers and C-suite leaders understand that what inclusiveness demands is actually a mindset and skill set that fosters strong, effective leadership. Inclusive-minded people have skills and attributes that are becoming the hallmarks of leadership:

courage

curiosity

commitment

collaboration

communication

cognizance of bias

cultural intelligence

managing diverse teams

Keep in mind that inclusiveness as a leadership competency is not reserved for people with titles like "diversity officer" or "inclusion manager." Framing inclusion as a leadership competency at all levels will be especially helpful in achieving buy-in from managers or career-focused individuals who might see D&I efforts as a potential distraction.

On the contrary, participation in D&I initiatives opens the door to valuable new skills and upward mobility.

At the same time, those already in top leadership roles might need to be similarly educated on the value of developing inclusion-minded leadership teams. They should be encouraged to add inclusiveness to their benchmarks for well-rounded potential leaders. Some organizations, such as The Carter Group Inc. of Mobile, Alabama, which provides management training and development programs, have shifted away from cross-cultural approaches to training and toward promoting soft skills that support inclusion.[14]

When companies broaden the concept and outcomes of D&I to include leadership, employees can become a constructive part of championing work that moves the whole organization forward. For current leaders who've built their careers in more homogeneous environments, an inclusive-minded approach is critical to continued success in a changing environment.[15]

#3 DON'T GET PERSONAL

The individual experiences and preconceptions that people bring to diversity work are numerous and can be the source of backlash. Honest D&I work uncovers people's anxieties and advantages, and this might provoke strong emotions. Even as we work to create space for individuality and openness about the challenges faced by specific groups, it's best to avoid creating tension by getting too personal.

Of course, people's personal lives and experiences inside and outside of work are often entangled. The trick is to acknowledge firsthand experiences without focusing on them when implementing D&I initiatives.

For example, after feedback showed that people disliked personal issues being a focus in its diversity curriculum, the University Corporation for Atmospheric Research amended its workplace diversity program to acknowledge external challenges that can impact work performance, advancement, and career choice. Yet, it avoided covering explicitly personal topics such as parenting choices. The research institution also found that people wanted to discuss inclusion at all levels, which presumably made the experience feel more organizationally focused.[16]

Reiterating the business impact is another method of helping people understand that although they might be affected by D&I initiatives, they are not targets. Additionally, the focus on workplace issues makes it easier to create and implement an action plan that people can support and participate in.

We also need to focus on cultural competence, not political correctness. When groups have a heightened level of intelligence about other cultures, they possess the vocabulary to help them understand and even advocate for a group or an inclusion practice — without focusing on individual people's personal feelings.

> *When everyone understands how D&I helps your organization do its work better, they'll be more eager to make D&I a daily reality.*

#4 BE HONEST

Research has shown that D&I initiatives can make some people feel uncomfortable, even threatened.[17] One of the most important parts of achieving buy-in among various groups is acknowledging the anxiety they might feel about this work.

Majority Anxiety

White men, for example, have exhibited a physiological threat response in mock interview scenarios at the very mention that the company was committed to diversity.[18] It turns out that a growing body of evidence indicates that white men — often the workplace majority — feel attacked, left out, and anxious when faced with a stated commitment to prioritizing diversity and inclusivity.

Minority Anxiety

People of color and others who are the intended beneficiaries of inclusion programs have fears of their own. A survey of 3,000 employees in 20 large U.S. organizations with stated commitments to diversity revealed that 40 percent refrained from behavior commonly associated with their own ethnic group. In addition, 29 percent changed their attire, grooming, or mannerisms to make their identity less obvious. They also limited contact with their own identity group and stayed silent when observing discriminatory treatment.[19]

People of color can feel significant anxiety when, after working to diminish their difference, a diversity initiative now puts it front and center.

All groups are less likely to resist D&I initiatives, however, when these emotions are acknowledged openly. Be honest about feelings that inclusion "takes something away from" dominant groups; admit they might experience a more competitive workplace once access and opportunity are spread equitably. Similarly, recognize underrepresented groups' feelings of vulnerability. However, be frank about the fact that D&I is not just about them – it's about a better workplace for everyone.

Honesty also includes transparency about every step of the process. Unfortunately, perceptions of D&I work have been damaged by several years of diversity initiatives that might need to be undone, and problems have often stemmed from a lack of transparency. To combat false preconceptions, offer clear definitions of what is happening. Another way help prevent a backlash against diversity initiatives is to explain the fundamental differences between diversity and affirmative action. For starters, make it clear that diversity doesn't rest on quotas or special treatment.[20]

By prioritizing transparency, you can help everyone realize that rather than disempowering them, diversity and cultural intelligence can empower them to improve their organization in meaningful ways.

#5 BE BOLD

Being bold about D&I means tackling unconventional issues or using unconventional methods. It's become too easy and, unfortunately, too common for D&I to become a "check-the-box" part of doing business. But when we boldly step outside of our expected areas of influence to address a larger social conversation, it signals a serious commitment.

One way is to boldly address the diversity issues that are more than gender- or skin-deep. Generation, educational background, parental status, age, and more can be sources of workplace inequity. It is increasingly important to boldly speak in terms of intersectionality, or the many facets of a person's lived experience or identity. This means resisting the urge to view stakeholders through just one dimension, even if that makes D&I work more complicated to define and execute.

You can also encourage your organization to be bold in publicly addressing issues. Corporations and other influential community organizations can change the larger social conversation deliberately or inadvertently, so they have a bigger responsibility than they think. True leaders take risks. When leaders who are not necessarily known as activists leverage their platforms to exert their influence, they often have an enormous impact on the way society or the community responds to an issue.

#6 ACTIVATE (CHEER)LEADERS

One of your biggest challenges – and potential successes – will be getting the highest levels of leadership to get behind your cause. However, it is crucial that CEOs, presidents, directors, etc., are visibly and vocally supportive of D&I initiatives.

You also need to make sure your entire leadership team physically embodies your goals. It goes without saying that this team should be as diverse and inclusive as possible. This isn't just about optics: You'll get direction from people who see every aspect of the picture, from costs to how distinct groups will be affected to considerations for implementation.

In order to attract and keep the best cheerleaders on your team, be sure to do the following:

- Be clear about what you need from each person. People need to know both the importance of their role within the organization and any personal leadership traits they bring to the effort.

- Go as high up the chain as you can. Take the initiative to educate yourself about what stakeholders need to hear in order to break through resistance.

- Explain how deliverables will be defined and measured, so everybody has a clear understanding of success.

- Avoid assumptions. Don't assume that people will want to take on extra work for personal reasons, such as appearing to identify with a particular identity group. Your best champions might not be who you think.

As the saying goes, be the change you want to see. The business case for D&I trickles down to every group in the organization, including your D&I team. That means in order to ensure your own success, you'll want a team that adheres as closely as possible to the culture, standards, and practices you hope to foster.

> *Some people quit because of slow progress, never grasping the fact that slow progress is progress nonetheless.*

STARTING WITH SELF

Getting active support from stakeholders such as majority and minority groups, organization leaders, managers, customers, and other constituents can feel like an unwieldy challenge. That tension is part of the unspoken work of D&I leadership. However, making use of the six secrets listed here and planning responses ahead of time can go a long way toward ensuring long-term success.

Sometimes we end up feeling alone in this work. Whether the reason is a lack of resources beyond our control or our own failure to reach out for needed support, prioritizing buy-in can be a helpful remedy. It might be necessary to address one group or issue at a time to show that buy-in can produce tangible results and is worth the investment.

At every stage, seek out those who can help you get the right information. Reevaluate whether each task is best performed by you as a diversity leader, or whether it should be delegated to someone else. Always consider how to bring as many people into the fold as possible.

Also, be sure that before you approach anyone else with the arguments and attitudes outlined here, you've mastered them yourself. D&I leadership requires a high level of self-awareness and intentionality. While we're working with intentionality, we also need to embrace flexibility.

"One size fits all" is perhaps the worst possible approach do D&I initiatives. It's great to research what has worked for other organizations, but resist the temptation to try and implement a cookie-cutter program. Every context is truly unique, and skilled D&I practitioners are willing to balance the universal principles of diversity, inclusion, and equity with the idiosyncratic needs of each organization.

Not only are organizations distinct, but so are the needs of individuals and stakeholder groups. One organization, UNEION, found through trial and error that structure was needed only at certain times when delivering D&I curriculum content. They reserved set content for introductions and tailored readings and activities based on a survey given to each cohort in advance. The result is that each group gets what they truly want and need and are empowered through the participation process.

How do you know when to prioritize flexibility? Start by simply asking your stakeholders about their needs and desires. That way, as you mindfully work to generate buy-in, you can be clear that your own motivations are driven by the needs of the organization.

With that mindset, you can be confident when acting boldly and honestly, and you yourself are a shining example of inclusive leadership. In this way, you can help bring lasting change to your organization and immeasurable improvement to yourself.

Always consider how to bring as many people into the fold as possible.
But first, master the mindset yourself.

Chapter 3
Activity vs. Impact

An interesting challenge arises when an organization begins to take steps toward becoming more diverse and inclusive. With the best of intentions, the person tasked with leading D&I often feels the need to show results — fast. They often end up creating a laundry list of activities to undertake.

You probably already know: Impact trumps activity every time.

Still, in the midst of our work, it can be hard to put this principle into practice. So, we continue undertaking various types of group programming, changing documented practices or policies, organizing feel-good social events, requiring sensitivity trainings, and more. In the rush to be progressive — or maybe react to a crisis — people fail to see the pitfalls of the activities they plan to undertake.

Even when organizations claim D&I is a goal, they fail to measure impact in this area the way they do other strategic goals, even though there are several ways to do so.[21] Part of the problem is a lack of clarity about what impact looks like. All too often, practitioners are dealing in a world of vague targets, so a completed to-do list eventually becomes a substitute for performance indicators. In the process, people who started out sincerely wanting to make change become so busy with activity that they forget or fail to consider impact.

DEFINING IMPACT

Simply put, impact is the goal, and activity is the way to reach it. The Institute for Diversity Certification (IDC) offered a definition of "impact" in its 2016 CDE Exam Study Guide:

> **Impact** is quantifiable or potential change in one or more key areas, including the economic, environmental or cultural, personnel and legal arenas.

> **Measuring impact** means figuring out what knowledge an activity introduces and how that knowledge is applied. Impact manifests as attitude and behavioral changes that make for a more inclusive environment.

On the most basic level, impact can be measured in terms of demographic diversity, though organizations need to make sure they're using appropriate measurement tools.[22] Beyond that, impact means making a difference in real people's lives and in the culture of an organization. It often means making believers out of unbelievers, which is important for such complex issues as D&I.

To be clear, activity is good. It's a signal to stakeholders that you are serious about D&I, and it gives people opportunities to engage and learn. Yet the danger in activity is that any movement feels so good that each step might seem to be a complete operation in and of itself.

ENSURING IMPACT

In the best-case scenario, D&I activities begin in the planning phase with clear impact goals. Such planning includes assessing attitudes or behaviors before and after group activities occur. These assessments help measure impact and can also help shape the activity to make sure it addresses all relevant needs. Specifically, assessments help you understand knowledge gaps, how new knowledge is being applied, and any resulting changes in attitude or behavior.

Another way to ensure desired impact is to figure out ahead of time what structures need to be in place in order for an activity to lead to impact. That includes communication. Besides the immediate details, stakeholders need to know how the activity fits into a bigger, long-term effort and what their own responsibilities are to contribute to its success.

Even if activities are already underway or complete, it's not too late to increase their impact. D&I practitioners can still work to understand how previous experiences categorically affected participants or subsets of an organization. The most responsive or enthusiastic respondents can also be tapped to help brainstorm a concerted follow-up effort, define the end goals, and determine how success will be measured to refine future initiatives.

Adding this deeper level of work to D&I activity can be challenging. However, approaching the work with the goal of tangible, positive impact creates a level of accountability that pays off over the long term. As good as activity feels today, it cannot compare to the deep satisfaction that comes with knowing that lasting change has impacted individual people's lives and the organization at large.

#1 POLICE YOUR POLICIES

Activity: Revise one or more policies.

One of the go-to D&I activities for many organizations is to create or revise policies in order to change behaviors. This often occurs in response to a crisis or to head off an issue that has gained public attention. The problem with policies is the approach organizations take time and time again: a problem occurs, management calls for new policies or mandatory training to "check the box," and that's the end of it. But box-checking alone can worsen interpersonal conflict or give a dangerous impression of insincerity.[23]

Impact: Connect policies to goals and keep communicating.

Any policy changes must be clearly connected to the goals of the organization and its individuals.[24] This helps ensure that policies accomplish meaningful, measurable change and creates a transparency that fosters trust and greater buy-in and reduces resistance. People up and down the ladder need to understand how the new policies affect their division or team and their own individual roles.

Don't assume that people will connect the dots for themselves. Supervisors in particular must clearly know how their management style might need to change or adapt and what the incentives are to make those changes.[25]

Finally, make sure ongoing training is built into policy development. Like any other valuable information, such training needs to stay current. As staff turnover inevitably occurs, each new person who absorbs and contributes to the culture must be able to understand the importance of D&I policies so that they can successfully comply.

#2 RAISE THE BAR ON HIRING

Activity: Recruit diverse candidates.

It's good news when an organization is ready to tackle D&I challenges by recruiting from underrepresented groups. Most try to reach this goal by posting jobs in places that may better reach diverse groups, or they may engage outside firms to help with recruitment. Without the proper foundation, however, such activities have a negligible impact.

Impact: Conduct an inclusive culture audit and implement changes as needed. To ensure that your efforts to recruit diverse candidates create a positive economic and cultural impact in addition to demographic changes, a culture audit should be the very first step. A culture audit would be similar to any other research exercise the organization might undertake. Specific goals need to be set, and then D&I leaders should spend time investigating in depth how to reach those goals.

This effort should include both quantitative and qualitative approaches. Quantitative approaches include simply looking at the hard numbers on hiring within the organization, incorporating industry or sector data on underrepresented groups.[26]

Qualitative information is readily available. A focus group of current employees would yield valuable information about current challenges and opportunities. D&I leaders can also gather focus groups of people who have left the organization. Additionally, the recruitment process can be amended to poll new candidates or prospects about their perceptions of D&I at the organization.

#3 ENERGIZE YOUR EVENT ATTENDANCE

Activity: Attend a supplier diversity fair.

A supplier diversity fair, which allows networking with small, women-owned, or minority-owned businesses, can be a terrific opportunity to learn about new purchasing options for every type of resource your organization needs while being inclusive. However, many visitors fail to take full advantage of the activity, leaving with little more than a list of contacts and a handful of marketing materials that makes little difference in their organizations.

Impact: Ensure processes enhance diverse vendors' visibility.

In order to turn a supplier diversity fair visit into something that creates a meaningful, measurable change in your organization, the real work needs to happen back at the office.[27] Before even attending the event, make sure the appropriate systems or processes are in place to add new prospects to the pool of considered options. An existing centralized list may need updating, or the information might be somehow dispersed throughout the organization.

After that, set diversity-oriented goals for employees in charge of buying. Robust organizations not only track and increase supplier diversity, but also reach out to enable diverse suppliers to win their business.

For example, Google created a tool to help buyers throughout the company find smaller companies that could be flying under the radar. The company expanded its definition of underrepresented companies, promised detailed responses to online inquiries within two weeks, and instituted a training program to improve small suppliers' business skills.[28]

Smaller organizations can find outside help for organizing supplier relationships, such as regional chapters of the National Minority Supplier Development Council.

#4 PLAN FOR PERSONNEL

Activity: Create a diversity officer position.

It often happens that organizations create a diversity officer position in response to a crisis or other pressing matter that's received public attention. With this reactionary approach, they neglect to put into place the necessary elements for the newly hired or promoted person to be successful in the role or for the role to remain meaningful over the long term.

Impact: Create a resource and succession plan for diversity officers.

Even the most capable and enthusiastic person is going to need a strong suite of resources to successfully move the needle on D&I.[29] Those resources include funds, visible leadership participation, supporting personnel, access to information, and clear authority. When these elements are missing, so is the opportunity for long-term impact.[30]

Similarly, the position needs a clear succession plan. Too often, organizations create a D&I position and engage an enthusiastic employee, but then the role disappears once that person moves on to another role or company. When that happens, their ideas often leave with them. If the role isn't left vacant, as is often the case, the replacement person ends up rebuilding from scratch. The solution is to build in a succession plan at the same time the position is created. Make sure there are clear answers to questions such as:

- How are we creating a sustainable structure so that if the person in this role walks out the door, D&I don't walk out with them?

- From what pool will replacement personnel be drawn? What resources are dedicated to engaging more than one champion in these efforts?

- In what department will the budget for D&I programming and personnel be permanently housed?

#5 CHECK UP ON CELEBRATIONS

Activity: Celebrate popular cultural holidays.

All year long, the calendar offers easy opportunities to celebrate diverse groups. From Chinese New Year and Disability Independence Day to Black History, Women's History, and Autism Awareness months, annual check-ins with minority populations could fill a D&I practitioner's schedule. The problem is that these types of activities come with an end date, while D&I work must be treated as a continuous, sustainable initiative.

Impact: Treat cultural celebrations as entry points, and plan follow-up.

The solution is not to discontinue celebrations, but rather treat them as entry points rather than end goals. Before the event is even planned, discern plausible next steps. Decide on the desired, actionable takeaways, and plan for assessments to determine whether those goals were met.

These decisions should be based on an organization's specific needs, so it will require working with leadership to help determine current barriers to D&I. For example, cultural celebrations can be gateways to examining what barriers are keeping that group out of higher-level roles. The celebration could open the door for a formal support program for the celebrated group or continued intercultural engagement. Execution will be highly influenced by the nuances of the organization, but the main point is that impactful follow-up be planned as part of any cultural celebrations.

LONG-LASTING IMPACT

With just the handful of examples listed here, D&I champions can boost the impact of popular activities and offer continuity to existing efforts. Recall that impact is measurable change for real people. It may change their economic reality, working environment, or the company's larger culture and personnel makeup. Simply celebrating a culture or checking out diverse suppliers will not make those kinds of changes in an organization. Even more involved activities such as changing policies, recruiting diverse candidates, and creating D&I leadership positions will fail to create a lasting impact if they do not take place on a foundation built for impact.

D&I leaders must always work toward lasting impact for any activities. Activities must fit into a larger structure of clearly defined goals or serve as a way to better understand and act upon an organization's specific needs. This can be a challenging way to approach D&I work, especially having expended a sincere effort on activities already. But approaching the work with an eye toward tangible, positive impact creates a level of accountability that pays off in the long term.

> *Gaining traction makes the journey so much more exciting and fulfilling. Position yourself to be impactful so you can celebrate those milestones to keep you going and energize your work.*

Chapter 4
The Complex Key: Intersectionality

DEFINING INTERSECTIONALITY

In its most basic definition, intersectionality is the interrelatedness of multiple identity categories such as age, gender, class, race, and ability. However, the concept is most often raised in discussion of the negative impacts of those interrelated identities. As a result, most definitions resemble something like the following:

> The interconnected nature of social categorizations such as race, class, and gender as they apply to a given individual or group, regarded as creating overlapping and interdependent systems of discrimination or disadvantage.
> (Google Dictionary)

> The complex, cumulative way in which the effects of multiple forms of discrimination (such as racism, sexism, and classism) combine, overlap, or intersect, especially in the experiences of marginalized individuals or groups.
> (Merriam-Webster Dictionary)

Intersectional theory has been principally developed in the academic sociology realm over the past several decades. Among the fields of study that have most actively expanded upon intersectionality are women's and gender studies, race studies, and cultural studies. At the same time, larger societal movements such as the civil rights movement, the women's rights movement, and Black Lives Matter have also highlighted intersectionality in their activism. In all of these arenas, the principal argument is that correcting inequity requires a multifaceted view of how members of the target group experience the world.

WHY INTERSECTIONALITY MATTERS FOR D&I

Although it has taken some time for the concept of intersectionality to break out of academic circles, it is now finding its way into major business conferences and individual organizations.[31] While we all have a natural human tendency to assign individuals to simple categories, the reality is that identities overlap, compound, and even evolve over time.

Deloitte lays out one business-focused explanation of why one-dimensional D&I efforts are simply not enough:

> Any attempt to bucket groups for D&I initiatives is incomplete as
> a diversity framework, because any such effort forces the choosing
> between identities and the privileging of one identity over others.
> Put another way, the very act of naming or categorizing group

identities has the paradoxical effect of excluding or downplaying other intersecting identities of the individual members of that group.[32]

However, the powerful fact that identifying with one category excludes other parts of one's identity is constantly overlooked or minimized when it is acknowledged. While people are often able to recognize and discuss the complexity of their own identities, they are much less likely to recognize or acknowledge the same in their coworkers. This can make it difficult to understand problems on your team, and it can blind leaders to hidden potential among groups and individuals.

Adopting an intersectional lens might call for a radical reframing of D&I within an organization or within your own mind. It brings to the fore questions such as:

- In an atmosphere where everyone appears to look alike, does that mean there is no diversity?
- When more people who look different are brought in, does that mean the work is done?
- Can affinity groups truly serve people if they are based on single categories?
- Are affinity groups inadvertently or inherently exclusive?

At the same time, recognizing intersectionality creates a wealth of opportunities for understanding how people can be their very best by bringing their whole selves to work. When we understand the multifaceted strengths and challenges that people bring to our organizations, we also gain a better picture of how our teams can excel because of these individuals.

I have witnessed and experienced firsthand how, when you're able to open up and allow yourself to be vulnerable, sharing narratives about your experiences helps people to really understand the lens through which you view life. It positions people to become a little more sensitized to your fight or your perspective. It humanizes individuals. There is a powerful humanizing effect to openly exploring our intersectional realities.

USING YOUR INTERSECTIONAL LENS

The numerous categories of difference in the workplace can intersect in countless ways. It can depend on everything from the type of industry to the makeup of the personnel. Below are some examples that illustrate the complexity that becomes apparent when examining inequity through an intersectional lens. In each case, consider the ways in which certain identities can heighten the experience of marginalization in the workplace as well as the opportunities they create for unlocking the power of inclusion.

1. Age, Gender, and Technology

One study in the health-care industry found that as workplace technology changed, older workers prone to experiencing age bias had to compensate in additional ways that were invisible to their employers.[33] For instance, they might spend extra time working at home to complete tasks, or spend more time outside of work exercising in order to keep up with the physical demands of their jobs. Others either sought early retirement or moved into positions where being older was no longer a disadvantage.

At the same time, lower-level managers were making accommodations so that older workers could remain on the job. In contrast to attitudes among the most senior-level managers, they found little issue with accommodations such as daytime-only rotating shifts or shorter shifts for older workers or allocating various tasks that didn't challenge limitations due to age.

The intersectional examination in the study also uncovered a gendered aspect of age and technology changes. While age impacted everyone, different accommodations were made for positions that were dominated by men versus positions that were dominated by women. Specifically, aging doctors (mostly male) received more accommodations than aging nurses (mostly female).

2. Nationality and Ethnicity

Intersectionality is also important in examining compounding identities related to nationality and ethnicity. One study found that when looking at immigrant populations, the nature of their immigration to the country made a difference in how effective unions could be when advocating for the group.[34] Because trade unions tend to consider migrants primarily as workers rather than as migrant workers with particular and overlapping forms of oppression, they tend to see workplace and migration issues as separate. Failing to realize the intersectionality of the experiences of migrant workers affected recruitment strategies and activities, hindering the effective involvement of diverse and marginalized workers in unions.

Another study examined how ethnicity and class or economic status can have significant compounding effects at many stages of employment. A study in the United Kingdom found that ethnic minorities were less likely than white majority group members to have jobs that provided them with pensions. What's more interesting is the study revealed that even when ethnic minorities do gain employment with pension benefits, some groups – specifically Pakistani, Bangladeshi, and Polish individuals – were much less likely to participate, and therefore fewer received the long-term benefits for various reasons.[35]

Viewed through a conventional lens, whites or white men would have been seen as a monolithic group. But the intersectional lens the researchers took recognized that the Polish were an ethnic minority group within that society. As a result, differential impacts and experiences among this subgroup were revealed. (And, when broken down even further, Pakistani, Bangladeshi, and Polish women had significantly different outcomes from their male counterparts.)

3. Race and Gender

The compound impacts of racial minority status and gender can leave women of color at the farthest edges among marginalized or underserved groups. Organizations are starting to acknowledge that women of color face multiple challenges when trying to break into environments dominated by white males. One black woman explained why black males have more access than people like her: "We're not guys and we don't look like them, so it's hard for white men in tech to empathize with us."[36]

Silicon Valley software company Slack was famously one of the first among its peers to publicly examine intersectionality. In its 2016 report, the company stated:

> *Often not reported among tech companies is the intersection of race and gender. Looking at women within underrepresented people of color (Native, Black, Hispanic/Latina, also frequently referred to as underrepresented minorities or "URMs") we found that 9% of our engineering organization in the US report in these categories.*[37]

That recognition was only the beginning. Since then, the company and its peers in the tech sector have continued to work on maintaining an intersectional approach, and responding accordingly has been an ongoing work.

4. Class and Gender

While sexual harassment is a well-known problem throughout the working world, women with lower-status jobs within an organization can be much more susceptible and unprotected than others. Additionally, women's experiences can vary across industries. As one author discussing the hospitality industry put it, "The dynamics of harassment against women breaking into the 'bro' culture of Silicon Valley are not exactly the same as the hostile working conditions for women pioneers in construction."[38]

Through anecdotal evidence, the author found that women in roles such as housekeeper, server, and casino card dealer often wield a very small amount of power to address problems in the workplace, due in part to biases against people with "low-skill" jobs. People tend to consider women in such jobs as lower-class as well, compounding the unbalanced power dynamic between genders in a way that women in corporate roles in the same companies would not experience.

5. Disability, Race, and Gender

People with disabilities are usually lumped together as a single group when, in fact, individuals can have significantly different workplace experiences depending on their specific type of disability. Using data from the U.S. Equal Employment Opportunity Commission (EEOC) Americans with Disabilities Act (ADA) Research Project, researchers discovered that intersections among disability, gender, race, and age made a significant difference in the risk of experiencing disability harassment.[39]

The researchers examined how individuals who file charges of harassment differ from individuals who file other types of disability discrimination charges (e.g., hiring, firing, or reasonable accommodation). Their results showed that women minorities are more likely to file harassment charges. Additionally, people with behavioral disabilities were more likely to complain of harassment than those with physical disabilities.

Looking more closely at the data, it revealed that across sectors, Hispanic or multiracial women with behavioral disorders were the most likely by far to file disability harassment charges. Additionally, an even closer look revealed that in some sectors, Hispanic women with physical impairments were most likely to file harassment complaints.

INTERSECTIONAL LEADERSHIP

Intersectionality reveals D&I work to be more challenging than it might seem at first; however, developing an intersectional mindset can be a hugely valuable leadership competency. Not only does it allow you to better understand problems on your team, it can open your eyes to unrealized potential among groups and individuals.

Now that we know how an intersectional lens works toward better seeing and addressing D&I issues for all groups, what does it do for those of us charged with fixing those issues?

For one, it makes us more able to assess and build upon our own experiences. Leaders' efficacy is determined precisely by their intersectional realities, which include education, work experience, and values as well as their lived diversity experiences − race, gender, ethnicity, age, etc.[40]

What's more, Deloitte argues that "to move the dial with respect to traditional D&I and create a more inclusive corporate culture, it is important to train our leaders to recognize intersectionality by becoming more emotionally mature."[41] Intersectionality requires a high level of self-awareness, empathy, and self-regulation, qualities that help us look out for bias, redirect disruptive impulses, and be mindful of invisible identities. As an important part of the solution, the authors call on leaders to reflect on their own compound identities and share their own stories.

Because leadership development is crucial, an intersectionality assessment can and should be tied to leadership. For example, a particular team leader's results might show the following: Everyone on her team has the same Myers-Briggs profile; individuals on her team forfeited most of their vacation time last year; no requested flexible work arrangements or stretch assignments were granted; and everyone she is mentoring is a straight white female who went to an Ivy League school – just like her.[42] Where others might not see an issue, these are the kinds of characteristics that intersectional leaders would recognize as a red flag for further investigation.

Analytics will reveal the multidimensionality of a team and provide direction for the self-regulation quality highlighted earlier. Much of the work described here involves detailed research, but even an examination of how your organization treats identity categories can be a significant first step. Intersectionality should help inform planned or ongoing D&I initiatives where there might be gaps in service or opportunities for improvement. In the best-case scenario, it can reveal a whole "new" landscape in which individuals at all levels can do and be their best.

Open-door prompts like "Tell me more" or "Help me to understand" lead people to a place where they can begin to share eye-opening perspectives.

Chapter 5
Tricky Topic: Equity vs. Equality

While the needs and ideas around D&I continue to evolve, you've likely seen "equity" appear as part of the discussion. I would argue that equity is not an additional aspect of D&I, but rather a foundational one. At the same time, there is still a significant amount of confusion about what equity means and its role in the workplace. Is it the same as equality? Is it the same as fairness? How do we ensure equity? Why should we even try?

As a D&I practitioner at any level, it's absolutely crucial that the answers to these questions are clear in your mind.

A lack of equity in the organizational culture affects how resources are prioritized. Looking at how — or if — various groups have access to resources such as funding, space, contact with leaders, or opportunities for advancement can help break cycles that perpetuate inequity. Addressing the issues can boost peoples' chances for success.

No matter the organization, the work of D&I cannot be successful without a consistent focus on equity.

Yet, that does not mean the concept will be an easy sell. For example, I find many people have a hard time wrapping their minds around the notion that serving the specific needs of certain groups does not mean the de facto exclusion of other groups. They raise questions such as, "When you have a minority business accelerator program, where you're only targeting minority individuals, aren't you excluding white people?"

Those are the times when it is necessary to go into a deeper conversation to help educate around the fact that so many circumstances have allowed for the severe disparities we see in our society. You'll need to help people understand that there are times when it's appropriate for us to try to level that playing field and to create a greater level of diversity and opportunity for all.

DEFINING EQUITY

So, how do we define equity?

First of all, equity is very different from equality, though people frequently confuse the two. While human beings should be considered equally valuable and worthy, that does not mean they should all be treated exactly the same way. Here is one way to begin thinking about or explaining the difference:

Equality is when everyone has access to the same thing.

Equity is when everyone has access to what they need to be successful.

And that's the thing that makes equity so tricky. What people need to be successful can vary from person to person and from one organization to another. Because equity can change depending on context, employers often back away from trying to resolve problems by addressing inequity. Instead, they try to be "fair." However, that approach rarely solves the problem at hand.

"Fair" doesn't always work for everybody.

One person who has brought public attention to the subtleties of equity is U.S. Senator Tammy Duckworth. As the first woman to give birth while in the Senate, she advocated for changes to a rule that bans children from the Senate floor.

At first glance, the standing rules were completely "fair." Nobody could have children with them on the Senate floor. Everybody had the same restriction. However, because infants need to be close to their parents for a variety of reasons, the fair rules meant that a large segment of current and potential senators may have their opportunities to participate limited if they have small children. With no accommodating facilities nearby, they wouldn't be allowed to perform their job if they needed to do it with a baby in tow. That created a barrier to inclusion.

EQUITY IN ACTION

The concept of equity becomes easier to grasp when looking at a variety of real-world examples. Many of the best examples come from the education sector, which is far ahead of business and other sectors when it comes to identifying and addressing inequity. Consider the following:

- The Head Start preschool program was created by the U.S. federal government to be administered at the state level decades ago. By its very name, it is clear the program is intended to cater differently to some students based on their needs. Participants achieve quantifiably better educational outcomes than their peers who do not participate in the program.

- Federally funded pre-college summer programs initiated for young people of color during the 1960s have helped improve graduation rates for that group.[43]

- While some companies are increasing their educational requirements, others are doing away with them entirely. The latter group includes Google, international accounting firm Ernst & Young, Penguin Random House, Hilton, Apple, Starbucks, Nordstrom, Bank of America, and Home Depot.[44]

There's also an argument to be made for a moral, or at least ethical, responsibility to do what we can for those in our midst who face disadvantages that limit their opportunities for success. That kind of motivation is readily accepted in education circles,[45] but can be much harder for some to swallow in the professional world.

EQUITY AND YOUR TALENT POOL

There are also practical reasons to make sure our organizations are equitable places. For one thing, choosing uniformity and equality over equity can hurt your talent pool. I find that a lot of key decision-makers err on the side of fairness and equality in the hiring process. However, they need to think more deeply about how they find talent, or they risk missing a great recruitment opportunity.

No matter what, you should always hire the best person for the job. But sometimes the basic criteria you're using may need to change. For example, many companies are moving away from educational attainment as baseline criteria. Education level as a requisite can lock out potentially excellent candidates who did not have access to higher education or who gained the needed experience through other avenues.

It might be necessary to create a plan for equitable employment by reviewing your organization's hiring criteria and policies (see actionable steps later in this section). You can also look at possible training initiatives, career development opportunities, and accommodations that might need to be made. Any of these would be a great start and should help build true equity and greater success in your organization.

Don't forget equity after people have been hired.

Even companies that have gone the extra mile to create a diverse applicant pool need to be mindful of whether successful applicants can succeed within the company. If somebody hired is the only one of their identity group – the only woman, the only differently abled – they could face challenges that can keep them from advancing. These challenges too often go unnoticed and unquestioned as members of underrepresented groups quietly leave in search of more inclusive environments.

LEGAL REALITIES

Sometimes, it's the fear of litigation that keeps organizations from addressing inequity in impactful ways. The truth is, there have been few significant legal challenges to corporate diversity initiatives. When they do happen, it's because employers have failed to make sure every employee understands the value, not just the group that directly benefits.

In one pending court case, a white middle manager at Eastman Kodak in Rochester, New York, brought a lawsuit against the company alleging that he was demoted for poorly handling the alleged harassment of a black subordinate by his other employees. He claimed that the company's new zero-tolerance discrimination policy was being used to discipline and terminate white employees unjustly.[46]

In another case, an employee at YouTube claimed his company canceled interviews and told hiring managers to completely exclude applicants who were not from underrepresented groups.[47] That lawsuit is also pending as of this writing.

As these incidents suggest, companies can and do take a wrong approach to equity efforts. A Connecticut fire department was found to have done just that in 2009, when it disregarded the results of promotion examinations after finding that white employees outperformed minorities. In an apparent effort to address inequity, the fire department decided not to promote white and Hispanic employees whose test results called for promotion because none of its black employees attained promotion-worthy scores. The department was afraid the test possibly revealed some kind of bias that would get them sued, so instead they chose not to acknowledge the results.[48] The courts, however, deemed that action illegal.

Rather than violate its own policy, the fire department should have transparently addressed the issue as a wake-up call to deeply reexamine the test and any other mitigating factors to see if it truly was biased and if so, determine a solution to address it.

LEGAL RISKS OF INEQUITY

While occasional legal challenges do arise, there is far more legal danger in failing to address inequity. Pay equity is one area in which employers should identify and address problems or possibly face lawsuits.[49]

The law firm Ogletree Deakins advises that employers may be at risk for pay discrimination claims if they:

- do not have proper policies, procedures, and processes in place that would prevent pay disparities from occurring or would provide an appropriate defense where there are disparities based on legitimate reasons;

- have policies and procedures that are not well designed; and/or

- do not take steps to follow or ensure compliance with their appropriate policies and procedures.

The firm says the smart approach is to analyze policies, procedures, processes, and data to identify pay disparities and weaknesses by:

- identifying potential pay disparities within appropriate job classifications;

- determining whether there are legitimate explanations for those disparities and/or taking steps to correct the disparities as appropriate; and

- identifying and correcting weaknesses in the company's systems so that the employer is protected from claims of pay disparity going forward.

This kind of detailed legal advice is no accident. Transgressions such as discriminatory hiring practices, inadequate accommodations for people with disabilities, race- and gender-based pay inequities, and more have left us with a raft of legal precedents that serve as a warning. These cases have changed the landscape of the workplace. Unfortunately, they have often served as the unwelcome starting point for D&I practitioners called to address problems. The better choice we can help our organizations make is to root out problems before they become civil liabilities.

In the search for secure solutions, never forget to count the true costs of unresolved inequity.

Taking Action Toward Equity

Policies can be powerful.

They can both create and inhibit equity within organizations. At the same time, when organizations undertake D&I initiatives just to comply with policies, the bare-minimum effort that usually results makes it hard to elevate D&I to the next level. Instead of stopping there, a more intentional approach is to determine whether policies are enabling an equitable and inclusive environment.

One study that looked at how policies affected men's and women's ability to balance work and family life found that "when the option is made available to them, the majority of respondents — regardless of gender or education level — opt for an egalitarian relationship."[50] Women's traditional decision to leave the workplace during childbearing years and men's prevailing decision to rely on their job in order to be the family breadwinner were often a reflection of limited options, not a reflection of what people felt they needed or desired. As the researchers put it in black and white, "for both men and women, current work-family arrangements are often suboptimal and result from a particular set of unsupportive workplace policies and practices."[51]

While working on major policy changes, you will no doubt find yourself using some public policy initiatives as a measuring stick. When looking at the broader issues of how public policies can inhibit or promote racial wealth inequities, consider how policies have historically impacted minority groups negatively. Celebrate the fact that we now have opportunities to not only create new equitable policies, but also examine existing policies to make sure they are equitable. Then, honor the past by taking action now to find a remedy.

It's an inescapable truth that such remedies are unlikely to treat or affect all people equally. For example, equitable policies may have had to disproportionately benefit specific minority groups in order to compensate for historical structural disadvantages while seeking to balance existing disparities.[52] However, the good news is that these are precisely the kinds of challenges that create opportunities for new or improved policies.

PLACES TO LOOK FOR INEQUITY

Opportunities to improve are everywhere.

First, leaders must adopt the mindset of being more sensitive to the fact that their employees didn't all take off from the same starting line. They need to recognize that in order to help each one be successful, the solution can't be "one size fits all."

Second, articulating goals and anticipated outcomes for target populations is critical to managing expectations and realistically assessing the impact that developing or altering a policy may have.[53]

The more complex an organization, the more cracks there are for equity to slip through. The following are three common areas:

External Partnerships

Many organizations rely on outside partnerships in order to conduct business. A closer look might reveal a lack of equity in those outside relationships. There might be blind spots around their approach to vendors or suppliers that are keeping them from having the chance to connect with minority or diversity-rich vendors.

It would be incredibly difficult to try and figure out on your own all the disadvantages your potential vendors face; it's much easier to connect with groups that you know are working to address those inequities. For example, Minority Business Accelerator programs at chambers of commerce in cities nationwide work to address equity issues that stifle growing companies headed by disadvantaged groups. They create a network that overcomes barriers such as limited access to capital or being left out of networks that generate procurement opportunities.

Employment Opportunity

Employee turnover can offer companies an ongoing opportunity to attain equitable employment practices. These opportunities can take the form of a review of criteria and policies, training initiatives, career development opportunities, and special accommodations.

Oppenheimer Funds, an asset management company, was recognized as one of the best companies for multicultural women in part for programs that cater to the diverse needs of several groups. The company has "business resource groups" that serve Asian, black, differently abled, Latinx, LGBTQ+, military, and women employees.

Compensation Gaps

In many organizations, significant pay gaps exist between privileged and other groups. One of the most visible examples is the gender pay gap. Remedying these disparities not only requires a change in policies — perhaps greater transparency, increased oversight, stricter criteria, or all of the above — but also actions that are, again, unequal.

Tech giant Salesforce, for example, moved to close its gender pay gap by spending $3 million in 2015 to equalize compensation across the company. It turned out that roughly the same number of men and women were impacted, suggesting that some groups of men were also being undercompensated.[54] In this case, the move to address inequity for one group turned out to have resolved hidden inequity for even more people.

PLANNING TO ADDRESS INEQUITY

Careful planning is important to ensure success. Once you've identified a problem, here are steps you can take toward solving it:

1. **Select the right personnel to lead the effort.**
   To address its pay gap problems, Salesforce hired its first-ever Chief Equality Officer.[55] (Despite its name, the position was created to address equity.) Organizations might need additional help from experienced D&I consultants who can conduct audits and even help implement solutions.[56]

2. **Review policies.**
   At this stage, every aspect of the issues in question will need to be examined with an open mind and a fine-tooth comb. Policy review will entail multiple steps and might uncover that it's actually a lack of appropriate policies that's contributing to inequity.

3. **Conduct an equity audit.**
   There's no single correct way to conduct an equity audit, but whatever tools are used should match the industry and company size in order to ensure the best results. Common steps in an equity audit include the following:

   ☐ Conduct a recruitment self-audit.

   ☐ Evaluate employee training, development, and promotion opportunities.

☐ Evaluate your compensation system, including bonuses and benefits, for industry competitiveness.

☐ Review your performance evaluation system and outcomes.

☐ Assess opportunity for employees to win commissions and bonuses.

☐ Assess internal communications language and delivery mechanisms.

☐ Review retention rates among various groups.

☐ Assess punitive policies and practices.

☐ Assess policies to monitor equitable practices.

☐ Implement changes as needed.

☐ Record the effects of all changes and adjust as needed.

SAMPLE EQUITY AUDITS AND POLICIES

While it is important that your organization's D&I initiatives are tailored to the unique needs of your workplace and industry, there exist numerous examples of effective policies. By glancing through a few of the examples listed, you can get a sense of needs among organizations, as well as how some important standards appear again and again, regardless of the context. The following can be a starting point or serve as supporting evidence for an equity policy you are working to implement.

As a starting point or supporting evidence for an equity policy you are working to implement, try samples such as the National Committee on Pay Equity Ten-Step Guide (2010),[57] Unifor's (Canadian union organization) Equity Audit Report (2017),[58] the Association of Faculties of Medicine of Canada's Equity and Diversity Audit Tool (2011),[59] and the Australian Institute of Architects' Gender Equity Policy (2013).[60] You may also run a web search for an example of an organizational racial equity audit request for proposal.[61]

THE BIGGER PICTURE

Equity is good for business.

Diverse teams make organizations more effective and more profitable – research supports this. If we're allowing talented people to struggle or eventually leave all in the name of equality, we're diminishing our organizational capacity in the process. By taking a more equitable approach – not by treating everyone exactly the same – your organization can enjoy these outcomes. On a more common-sense level, the business case for equity goes back to some sayings we have all heard:

"A rising tide lifts all boats."

"You're only as strong as your weakest link."

"Don't look down on somebody unless you are helping them up."

There's also a bigger mission here: How we operate as a society either offers the potential for everyone to have a great level of success — or it doesn't. The truth is, some people are not going to care at all about equity versus equality, but leaders who are inclusion-minded need to be sure their efforts really offer access to what individuals need to be successful — not access to the same resources across the board.

Conclusion
Next-Level You

By now, you're ready to move to the next level. How that happens will be unique to your goals and your situation.

Each one of the concepts explored in this book could lead the committed Intentional Inclusionist® down a long learning path, a journey I encourage you to take. You might consider taking a deep dive into just one concept at a time. Or, you might choose a specific area of your D&I work and see how all the concepts in this book apply for you. Either way, my hope is that you've found yourself energized, understood, and maybe even provoked while reading this book.

There's no doubt that some parts of this guide resonated with you more than others, and now is the time to reflect on which parts those were.

Did you find yourself having imaginary conversations with specific people in your organization as you considered attitudes that can challenge buy-in?

Were you intrigued by the idea of how mindfulness can clear obstacles in your own mind or allow you to be better positioned to understand others?

Did you cringe or become excited when learning how common D&I activities can miss the mark – and how they can be drastically improved?

Do you now appreciate being able to speak the language of equity and intersectionality as you explain to stakeholders how and why your work must go deeper?

As the landscape of D&I work continues to shift, so should our practice in response. We have a ripe opportunity in our hands as challenges multiply, while, at the same time, more people are coming to recognize D&I as an important part of how every organization operates. As noted earlier, younger generations are becoming much more amenable to taking D&I seriously, and it's up to us to lay the groundwork for their natural inclinations toward equity and inclusion to build upon as they become leaders.

Meanwhile, no matter what title we hold, we need to show up as leaders whenever possible. As a D&I practitioner, I have made it a point to ensure that my contributions add value to whatever type of environment or organization I am working in. In fact, that is a priceless method for increasing your influence. By just adding value in general, you gain a level of respect and appreciation for simply being at the table. Then, when you do have to have a delicate conversation related to D&I, you've already generated a level of trust with your colleagues. With that trust in place, it's so much easier to try to get someone to appreciate your perspective or remain open to the respectful dialog that leads to understanding.

That is the key. Even with a sweeping and optimistic perspective and all signs pointing toward greater D&I, we know that lasting change happens little by little as thousands of us show up every day to do our unsung work. It happens one conversation, one review, one event, one meeting, and one mindful moment at a time. For this reason, I encourage you to find the one actionable step in this book you can take immediately. Write it down, make a plan, and accelerate your journey toward becoming a more knowledgeable and effective diversity leader no matter what your role.

At end of the day, we do our work so that others can bring their whole selves to work, enabling the best possible teams and cultures.

That is our true calling as leaders. In the sometimes unglamorous day-to-day of D&I efforts, let's not forget ourselves. We cannot effectively manage others if we do not first manage ourselves. Likewise, we can never truly see the needs and potential among others in our organization if we do not first examine our own state of affairs and create a personal roadmap toward excellence. Accomplishing that takes knowledge, wisdom, grace, and a commitment to intentionality. No matter what your level of responsibility for D&I in your organization, your work as an Intentional Inclusionist® cannot help but bring positive, lasting change. Experience has shown me that this will be a change you see happening around you, and one that others will no doubt see happening within you.

About the Author

Dr. Nika White's professional career spans about 20 years as a diversity and inclusion practitioner, accomplished marketing communications executive, economic development leader, and community advocate. She finds inspiration at the intersection of business, diversity, and leadership and is a sought-after consultant, thought leader, and speaker on issues of team engagement, organizational leadership, strategic diversity, and intentional inclusion.

In 2017, Dr. White launched Nika White Consulting. Her recognitions include South Carolina Career Woman of the Year, U.S. Small Business Association's South Carolina Minority Business Advocate of the Year, and *Greenville Business Magazine*'s 50 Most Influential People. National recognitions include *The Network Journal Magazine*'s Top 40 Under 40 Leaders and *Diversity MBA Magazine*'s Top 100 Under 50 Executives. Dr. White is a graduate of the U.S. Chamber of Commerce Foundation's Institute of Organization Management and a Certified Diversity Executive through the Institute for Diversity Certification, which confers globally recognized professional credentials to diversity and inclusion practitioners. She is the author of *The Intentional Inclusionist*®, a book for leaders who desire to grow as inclusion-minded individuals and exercise their leadership to enhance the workplace, build communities, and have a positive impact on any circle of influence to which they belong.

www.nikawhite.com

References

[1] Tessa L. Dover, Brenda Major, and Cheryl L. Kaiser, "Diversity Policies Rarely Make Companies Fairer, and They Feel Threatening to White Men," *Harvard Business Review*, January 4, 2016, https://hbr.org/2016/01/diversity-policies-dont-help-women-or-minorities-and-they-make-white-men-feel-threatened.

[2] Tessa L. Dover, Brenda Major, and Cheryl R. Kaiser, "Diversity initiatives, status, and system-justifying beliefs: When and how diversity efforts de-legitimize discrimination claims," *Group Processes & Intergroup Relations* (2013), https://labs.psych.ucsb.edu/major/brenda/docs/Dover,%20Major,%20&%20Kaiser%202014.pdf.

[3] Tessa L. Dover, Brenda Major, and Cheryl R. Kaiser, "Diversity initiatives, status, and system-justifying beliefs: When and how diversity efforts de-legitimize discrimination claims," *Group Processes & Intergroup Relations* (2013), https://labs.psych.ucsb.edu/major/brenda/docs/Dover,%20Major,%20&%20Kaiser%202014.pdf.

[4] Frank Dobbin and Alexandra Kalev, "Why Diversity Programs Fail," *Harvard Business Review*, July–August 2016.

[5] John Kabat-Zinn, *Full Catastrophe Living: Using the Wisdom of Your Body and Mind to Face Stress, Pain, and Illness* (Bantam Books, 1990).

[6] "Mindfulness Meditation Reduces Implicit Age and Race Bias: The Role of Reduced Automaticity of Responding," *Social Psychological and Personality Science* 6, no. 3 (2015).

[7] D. J. Burgess, M. C. Beach, and S. Saha, "Patient Education and Counseling Mindfulness practice: A promising approach to reducing the effects of clinician implicit bias on patients," *Patient Education and Counseling* 100, no. 2 (2016): 372-376.

[8] Sai Sun, Ziqing Yao, Jaixin Wei, and Rongjun Yu, "Calm and smart? A selective review of meditation effects on decision making," *Frontiers in Psychology* (July 24, 2015), https://doi.org/10.3389/fpsyg.2015.01059.

[9] Moses M. Tincher, Lauren A. M. Lebois, and Lawrence W. Barsalou, "Mindful Attention Reduces Linguistic Intergroup Bias," *Mindfulness* 7, no. 2.

[10] Adapted from Mayo Clinic, Healthy Lifestyle, Consumer Health (https://www.mayoclinic.org/healthy-lifestyle/consumer-health/in-depth/mindfulness-exercises/art-20046356?pg=2) and from Mindful.org, Exercise: Investigating Judgments (this article was adapted from Dr. Bob Stahl's and Steve Flowers' book, *Living with Your Heart Wide Open*).

[11] Martha Frase-Blunt, "Thwarting the Diversity Backlash," *HR Magazine*, June 1, 2003, https://www.shrm.org/hr-today/news/hr-magazine/pages/0603agenda_diversity.aspx.

[12] Martha Frase-Blunt, "Thwarting the Diversity Backlash," *HR Magazine*, June 1, 2003, https://www.shrm.org/hr-today/news/hr-magazine/pages/0603agenda_diversity.aspx.

[13] Juliet Bourke and Bernadette Dillon, "The Six Signature Traits of Inclusive Leadership Thriving in a Diverse New World," *Deloitte Insights*, April 14, 2016, https://www2.deloitte.com/insights/us/en/topics/talent/six-signature-traits-of-inclusiveleadership.html.

[14] Martha Frase-Blunt, "Thwarting the Diversity Backlash," *HR Magazine*, June 1, 2003, https://www.shrm.org/hr-today/news/hr-magazine/pages/0603agenda_diversity.aspx.

[15] Juliet Bourke and Bernadette Dillon, "The Six Signature Traits of Inclusive Leadership Thriving in a Diverse New World," *Deloitte Insights*, April 14, 2016, https://www2.deloitte.com/insights/us/en/topics/talent/six-signature-traits-of-inclusiveleadership.html.

[16] Allison-Scott Pruitt, Carolyn Brinkworth, Joshua Young, and Kristen Luna Aponte, "5 Things We Learned About Creating a Successful Workplace Diversity Program," *Harvard Business Review*, March 30, 2018, https://hbr.org/2018/03/5-things-we-learned-aboutcreating-a-successful-workplace-diversity-program.

[17] Tessa L. Dover, Brenda Major, and Cheryl L. Kaiser, "Diversity Policies Rarely Make Companies Fairer, and They Feel Threatening to White Men," *Harvard Business Review*, January 4, 2016, https://hbr.org/2016/01/diversity-policies-dont-help-women-or-minorities-and-they-make-white-men-feel-threatened.

[18] Tessa L. Dover, Brenda Major, and Cheryl L. Kaiser, "Diversity Policies Rarely Make Companies Fairer, and They Feel Threatening to White Men," *Harvard Business Review*, January 4, 2016, https://hbr.org/2016/01/diversity-policies-dont-help-women-or-minorities-and-they-make-white-men-feel-threatened.

[19] Jessica Pettitt, *Good Enough Now: How Doing the Best We Can with What We Have Is Better Than Nothing* (Sound Wisdom, 2017).

[20] Martha Frase-Blunt, "Thwarting the Diversity Backlash," *HR Magazine*, June 1, 2003, https://www.shrm.org/hr-today/news/hr-magazine/pages/0603agenda_diversity.aspx.

[21] Marjorie Derven, "Measure Diversity and Inclusion for Maximum Impact," *T+D* 67, no. 12 (2013).

[22] Salomon A. Guajardo, "Workforce Diversity: An Application of Diversity Integration Indices to Small Agencies," *Public Personnel Management* 42, no. 1 (2013).

[23] Tessa L. Dover, Brenda Major, and Cheryl L. Kaiser, "Diversity Policies Rarely Make Companies Fairer, and They Feel Threatening to White Men," *Harvard Business Review*, January 4, 2016, https://hbr.org/2016/01/diversity-policies-dont-help-women-or-minorities-and-they-make-white-men-feel-threatened.

[24] "Link Diversity to Business Goals for Best Results," *HR Focus* 87, no. 1 (2010).

[25] Marjorie Derven, "Measure Diversity and Inclusion for Maximum Impact," *T+D* 67, no. 12 (2013).

[26] Maxine Williams, "'Numbers Take Us Only So Far': Facebook's Global Director of Diversity Explains Why Stats Alone Won't Solve the Problem of Organizational Bias," *Harvard Business Review* 95, issue 6 (2017).

[27] Jeffrey McKinney, "50 Top Companies for Supplier Diversity," *Black Enterprise*, May/June 2017.

[28] Adrianna Samaniego, Adam Gardner, Chris Genteel, and Leonard Greenhalgh, "How They Did It: Google's Innovative Approach to Supplier Diversity," *Logistics Management* 56, no. 10 (October 2017).

[29] Kathleen Wong (Lau), "Diversity Work in Contentious Times: The Role of the Chief Diversity Officer," *Liberal Education* 103, no. 3 (2017).

[30] Loretta L. C. Brady, "Where Does Your Organization Place Diversity?" *New Hampshire Business Review* 36, no. 12 (2014).

[31] Lauren Hepler, "Expanding the definition of diversity in the corporate world," *San Francisco Business Times*, June 14, 2018.

[32] W. Sean Kelly and Christie Smith, "What if the road to inclusion were really an intersection?" *Deloitte Insights*, December 11, 2014, https://www2.deloitte.com/insights/us/en/topics/talent/multidimensional-diversity.html.

[33] Susan Halford, Natalia Kukarenko, Ann Therese Lotherington, and Aud Obstfelder, "Technical Change and the Un/Troubling of Gendered Ageing in Healthcare Work," *Gender, Work & Organization* 22, no. 5 (2015).

[34] Gabriella Alberti, Jane Holgate, and Maite Tapia, "Organising migrants as workers or as migrant workers? Intersectionality, trade unions and precarious work," *International Journal of Human Resource Management* 24, no. 22 (2013).

[35] Athina Vlachantoni, Zhixin Feng, Maria Evandrou, and Jane Falkingham, "Ethnicity and Occupational Pension Membership in the UK," *Social Policy & Administration* 49, no. 7 (2015).

[36] Valentina Zarya, "Tech Companies Shouldn't Treat Race and Gender Separately," Fortune.com, July 12, 2016.

[37] Slack, "Diversity and Inclusion: An update on our data," 2016 Report, https://slackhq.com/diversity-and-inclusion-an-update-on-our-data-7af803cedae4.

[38] Ellen Mutari, "#MeToo in the Hospitality Sector: How sex, gender, and class intersect when workers routinely face sexual harassment," *Dollars & Sense*, issue 336 (May/June 2018).

[39] Linda R. Shaw, Fong Chan, and Brian T. McMahon, "Intersectionality and Disability Harassment: The Interactive Effects of Disability, Race, Age, and Gender," *Rehabilitation Counseling Bulletin* 55, no. 2 (2012).

[40] Agnes Richardson and Cynthia Loubier, "Intersectionality and Leadership," *International Journal of Leadership Studies* 3, no. 2 (2008).

[41] W. Sean Kelly and Christie Smith, "What if the road to inclusion were really an intersection?" *Deloitte Insights*, December 11, 2014, https://www2.deloitte.com/insights/us/en/topics/talent/multidimensional-diversity.html.

[42] W. Sean Kelly and Christie Smith, "What if the road to inclusion were really an intersection?" *Deloitte Insights*, December 11, 2014, https://www2.deloitte.com/insights/us/en/topics/talent/multidimensional-diversity.html.

[43] Lucius T. Outlaw Jr., "Commentary: Diversity, Excellence, and Equity: Recognizing Diversity, Educating for Excellence, Fostering Equity, Nurturing Achievement, Rewarding Merit," *Journal of Negro Education* 83, no. 4 (2013).

[44] Amy Elisa Jackson, "15 More Companies That No Longer Require a Degree – Apply Now," Glassdoor.com, January 15, 2018, www.glassdoor.com/blog/no-degree-required/.

[45] Lucius T. Outlaw Jr., "Commentary: Diversity, Excellence, and Equity: Recognizing Diversity, Educating for Excellence, Fostering Equity, Nurturing Achievement, Rewarding Merit," *Journal of Negro Education* 83, no. 4 (2013).

[46] Martha Frase-Blunt, "Thwarting the Diversity Backlash," *HR Magazine*, June 1, 2003, https://www.shrm.org/hr-today/news/hr-magazine/pages/0603agenda_diversity.aspx.

[47] Kirsten Grind and Douglas MacMillan, "YouTube Hiring for Some Positions Excluded White and Asian Men, Lawsuit Says," *Wall Street Journal*, March 1, 2018, www.wsj.com/articles/youtube-hiring-for-some-positions-excluded-white-and-asian-males-lawsuit-says-1519948013?tesla=y&mod=e2tw.

[48] "U.S. Supreme Court Rules That City Discriminated Against White Firefighters in Landmark Reverse Discrimination Case," *Blank Rome Employment, Benefits & Labor Alert*, August 2009, www.blankrome.com/publications/us-supreme-court-rules-city-discriminated-against-white-firefighters-landmark-reverse.

[49] Liz S. Washko, "Reducing the Risks of Pay Discrimination Claims: Employer Pay Equity Audits," *Our Insights*, Ogletree Deakins, February 3, 2016, ogletree.com/shared-content/content/blog/2016/february/reducing-the-risks-of-pay-discrimination-claims-employer-pay-equity-audits.

[50] David S. Pedulla, "How Workplace Policies Block Gender Equality," *World Economic Forum*, January 30, 2015, www.weforum.org/agenda/2015/01/how-workplace-policies-block-gender-equality/.

[51] David S. Pedulla, "How Workplace Policies Block Gender Equality," *World Economic Forum*, January 30, 2015, www.weforum.org/agenda/2015/01/how-workplace-policies-block-gender-equality/.

[52] Prosperity Now, "Racial Equity Policy Design and Advocacy: A Primer," 2017.

[53] Prosperity Now, "Racial Equity Policy Design and Advocacy: A Primer," 2017.

[54] Kris Dunn, "The Salesforce Pitch for Equity, Equality," *Workforce Magazine*, January/February 2017.

[55] Kris Dunn, "The Salesforce Pitch for Equity, Equality," *Workforce Magazine*, January/February 2017.

[56] Lee V. Gaines, "District 65 Hires Consultant to Conduct 'Equity Audit,'" *Chicago Tribune*, June 14, 2016.

[57] National Committee on Pay Equity Ten-Step Guide (2010), https://www.pay-equity.org/cando-audit.html.

[58] Unifor's Equity Audit Report (2017), https://www.unifor.org/sites/default/files/documents/document/equity-audit-report-en-web-final_20170730.pdf.

[59] The Association of Faculties of Medicine of Canada's Equity and Diversity Audit Tool (2011), https://www.afmc.ca/pdf/committees/AFMC_ Equity_ and_Diversity_Audit_-Tool_10MAY2011.pdf.

[60] The Australian Institute of Architects' Gender Equity Policy (2013), http://architecture.com.au/docs/default-source/about-us/gender-equity-policy.pdf?sfvrsn=0.

[61] Example of an organizational racial equity audit request for proposal, https://philanthropynw.org/resources/example-organizational-racial-equity-audit-rfp.

Made in the USA
Columbia, SC
24 February 2021